AVENGERS IN ACTION!

Editor Feyi Oyesanya
Designer Molly Kellond
Production Editor Siu Yin Chan
Senior Production Controller Mary Slater
Managing Editor Emma Grange
Managing Art Editor Vicky Short
Publisher Paula Regan
Art Director Charlotte Coulais
Managing Director Mark Searle

Designed for DK by Colin Williams
Reading consultant Maureen Fernandes
DK would like to thank Chelsea Alon at Disney and Jennette ElNaggar at DK US.

First published in Great Britain in 2026 by
Dorling Kindersley Limited
20 Vauxhall Bridge Road,
London SW1V 2SA

The authorised representative in the EEA
is Dorling Kindersley Verlag GmbH. Arnulfstr. 124,
80636 Munich, Germany

Page design copyright © 2026 Dorling Kindersley Limited
A Penguin Random House Company
10 9 8 7 6 5 4 3 2 1
001–355839–April/2026

© 2026 MARVEL

All rights reserved.
Without limiting the rights under the copyright reserved above, no part of this publication may be reproduced, stored in or introduced into a retrieval system, or transmitted, in any form, or by any means (electronic, mechanical, photocopying, recording, or otherwise), without the prior written permission of the copyright owner. No part of this publication may be used or reproduced in any manner for the purpose of training artificial intelligence technologies or systems. In accordance with Article 4(3) of the DSM Directive 2019/790, DK expressly reserves this work from the text and data mining exception.

A CIP catalogue record for this book is available from the British Library.

ISBN 978-0-2417-8769-4

Printed and bound in China

www.dk.com

This book was made with Forest Stewardship Council™ certified paper – one small step in DK's commitment to a sustainable future. Learn more at www.dk.com/uk/information/sustainability

Level 3

AVENGERS IN ACTION!

Written by Feyi Oyesanya

Contents

6	Meet the Avengers
8	The first Captain America
10	Meet the new Captain America
12	Captain Marvel
14	The Prince of Asgard
16	Ant-Man
18	The Hulk
20	The Black Panther

22	Master of martial arts
24	The Prince of Atlantis
26	Avengers HQ
28	Earth's Mightiest Heroes
30	Meet the Thunderbolts
32	The Winter Soldier
34	The Widows
36	Meet the Fantastic Four
38	The God of Mischief
40	The last Eternal Titan
42	Doctor Doom
44	Joining forces
46	Glossary
47	Index
48	Quiz

Meet the Avengers

These heroes are Earth's first line of defence. Some members of the team have special powers.

Some are trained to be strong fighters. They protect the world against the villains in the universe.

The first Captain America

Steve Rogers is the first Captain America. He works hard to keep the world safe.

Steve makes friends with another hero, Sam Wilson. He trains him to be a strong fighter. Steve loses his powers and asks Sam to take the shield. After he recovers, they both share the role of Captain America.

Meet the new Captain America

Sam Wilson is Captain America. He works with the Avengers on important missions. His new suit has large, red wings. This allows him to keep the streets and the skies safe. Sam is a brave hero. He loves protecting people from villains by soaring into action with his shield.

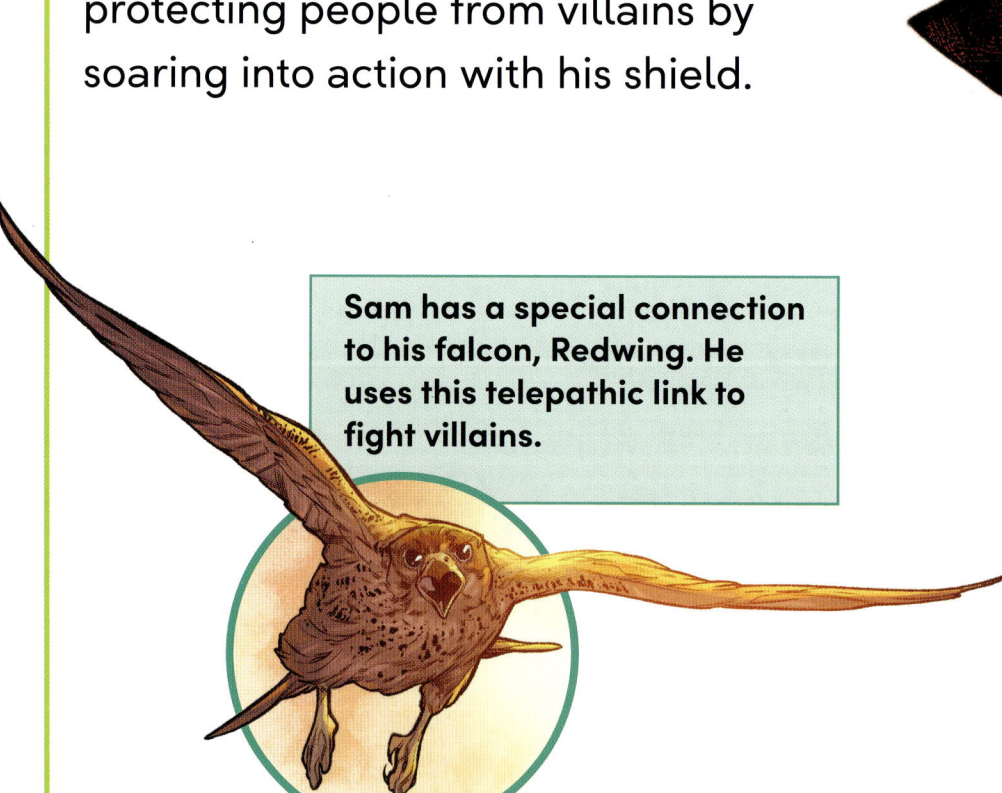

Sam has a special connection to his falcon, Redwing. He uses this telepathic link to fight villains.

Captain Marvel

Carol Danvers is one of the most powerful Super Heroes in the universe. She can fly into space and has superhuman strength. Carol joins the Avengers and names herself Captain Marvel.

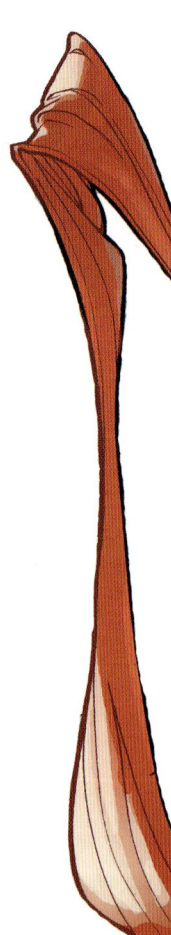

The Prince of Asgard

Thor is the Prince of Asgard, home of the Norse gods. He uses an enchanted hammer called Mjolnir to protect others. Thor's brother Loki tries to destroy him, but his allies on Earth come together to help. After the battle, this group of heroes call themselves the Avengers.

When Thor spins his hammer, he can fly.

Ant-Man

Hank Pym is the first Ant-Man. He can shrink to insect size and grow as tall as a giant. Hank meets a young man named Scott Lang and gives him his Ant-Man suit. Scott Lang becomes the next Ant-Man, and joins the Avengers.

Scott can change size with the power of his mind.

The Hulk

Bruce Banner is one of the best scientists in the world. He transforms into a large, green monster called the Hulk whenever he becomes anxious or angry. The Hulk has incredible strength and can jump great distances.

The Hulk is one of the founding members of the Avengers.

The Black Panther

T'Challa is the King of Wakanda, a small kingdom in Africa. He also protects Wakanda as the powerful warrior the Black Panther. He becomes an Avenger, and helps protect Earth too.

Master of martial arts

Shang-Chi is a martial arts master who wants world peace. He joins the Avengers for several missions. He uses internal energy to help him fight. This energy also helps him stay calm in tense situations.

The Prince of Atlantis

Namor is the Prince of Atlantis, an underwater kingdom in the North Atlantic Ocean. He is able to hear and talk to animals in the sea. He can also talk to his soldiers with his mind. Namor is powerful and tough. As a member of the Avengers, he battles against villains such as Thanos and Doctor Doom.

Avengers HQ

The Impossible City is a living city. A group of villains called the Ashen Combine force the city to work for them. When the Avengers defeat the villains, the city joins the team. The Avengers now use the city as their home in the sky.

While the rest of the Avengers were defeating the villains, Captain America and the Black Panther freed the city.

Earth's Mightiest Heroes

The Avengers are much more than a group of heroes with special skills. They bring people on Earth together, and give them hope.

Hawkeye
Clint Barton is an expert soldier. He is a great archer, and joins the Avengers to protect people.

Black Widow
Natasha Romanoff is the Black Widow. She is a trained super spy and a martial arts expert.

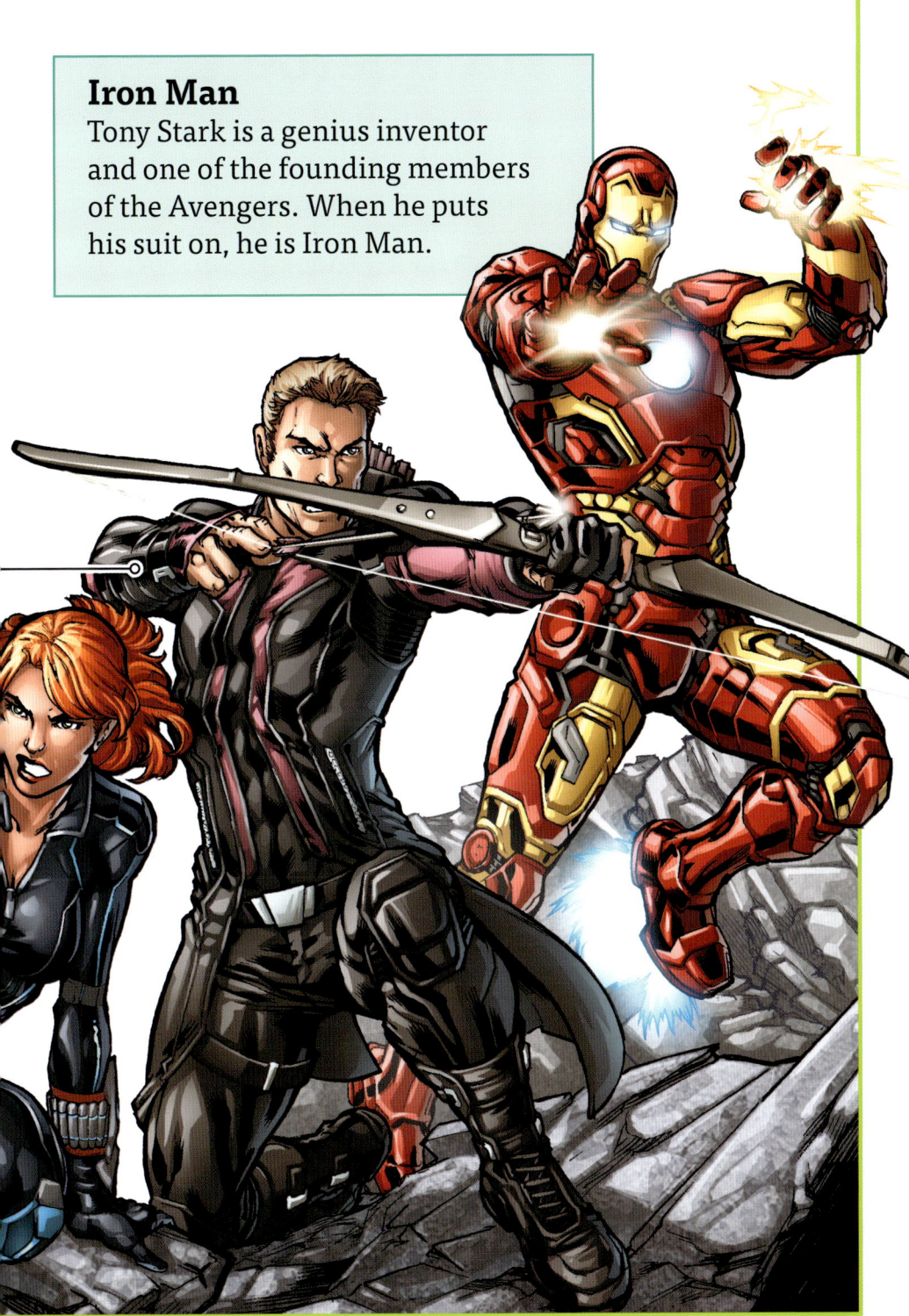

Iron Man
Tony Stark is a genius inventor and one of the founding members of the Avengers. When he puts his suit on, he is Iron Man.

Meet the Thunderbolts

The Thunderbolts team start as a group of antiheroes pretending to be heroes. After a while, the group stop pretending and become real heroes. The Thunderbolts prove that even the worst villains can put their pasts behind them.

The Winter Soldier

Bucky Barnes trains and fights with Steve Rogers. He serves as Steve's partner until he's captured on a mission. The enemy wipes Bucky's memories and forces him to become the Winter Soldier. Steve saves Bucky and returns his memories. Bucky decides to become a hero, and joins the Thunderbolts team.

The Widows

Natasha Romanoff is the first Black Widow. She trains to be a tough spy but becomes a hero instead. She is an Avenger. Yelena Belova also trains with Natasha to be a spy. She becomes the next Black Widow. Later, Yelena changes her mind and names herself the White Widow. She joins Bucky's Thunderbolts team on a few missions.

White Widow

Meet the Fantastic Four

The Fantastic Four sometimes work with the Avengers to help fight against villains, such as Doctor Doom. Mister Fantastic, the Invisible Woman, the Human Torch, and the Thing are incredibly brave. They love using their powers to help people as a team. However, their greatest powers might be their close family bond and their love for each other.

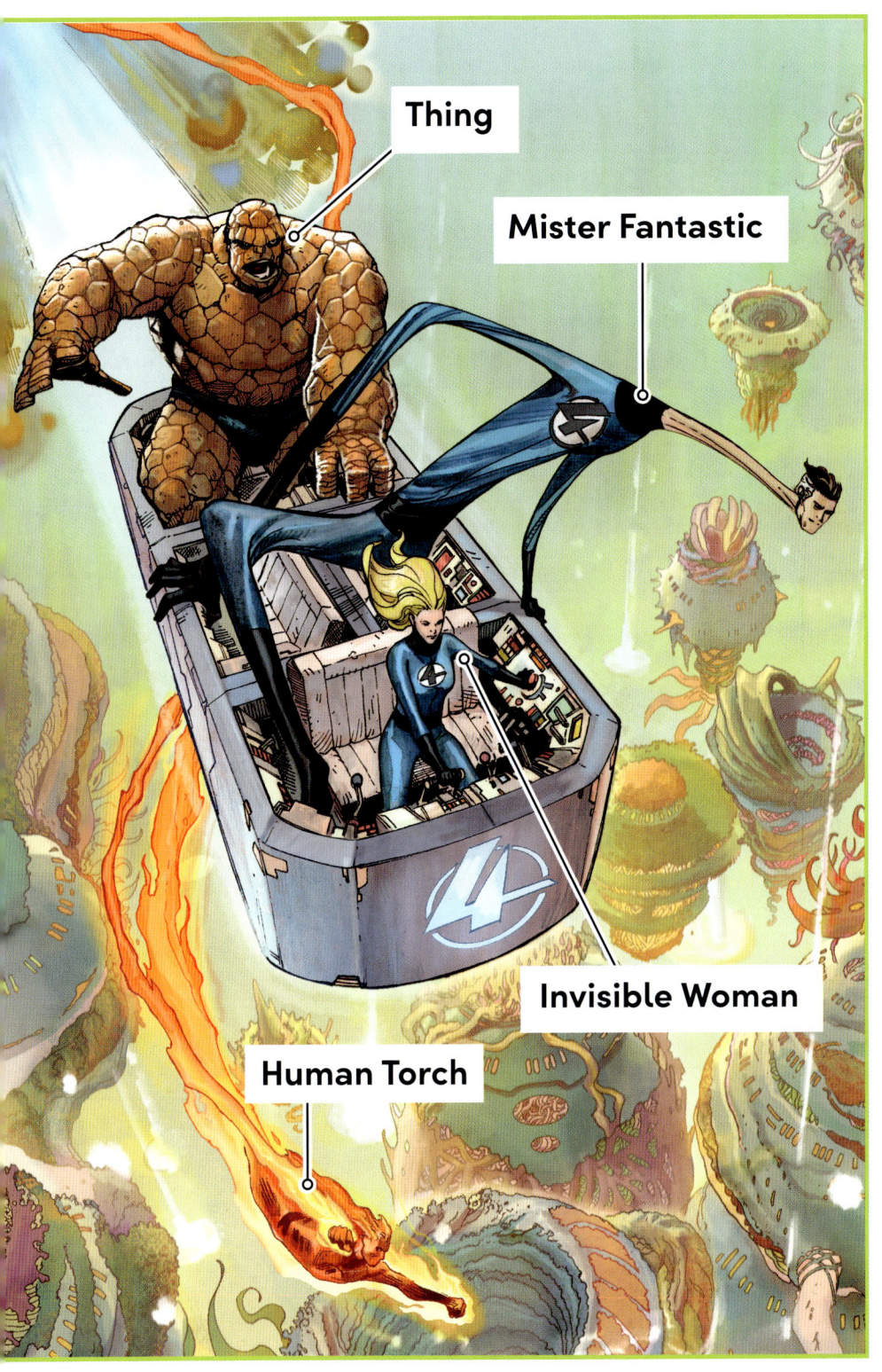

The God of Mischief

Loki is Thor's adopted brother. He is the god of mischief and evil. He can cast spells and transform into different people. As a child, Loki became jealous of Thor. This jealousy grew, and now Loki works hard to defeat Thor and the Avengers whenever he can.

The last Eternal Titan

Thanos is the last of the Eternal Titans, an alien race that existed a long time ago. He is powerful, and can channel this power through others. Thanos wants to control the universe and destroy the Avengers.

Doctor Doom

Doctor Doom is a genius scientist who craves power without limits. This dangerous villain works hard to take over the world. He has clashed with the Avengers on several occasions.

Doctor Doom wears a suit of armour and an iron mask to hide his face.

Joining forces

Although the Avengers and their allies have changed over time, the teams always work together. They help each other defeat the common enemy. As there is no shortage of villains, these heroes are always ready to jump into action!

Glossary

allies
people who help another person when they need it

anxious
feeling worried or nervous

archer
a person who uses a bow and arrows

connection
a link or bond between people or things

defence
when you protect yourself from harm

enchanted
filled with magic

genius
someone very, very smart

hero
a person who is admired for their bravery

inventor
a person who creates new things

martial arts
special fighting skills often used for self-defence

mischief
playful, harmless trouble

mission
a special task that someone is sent somewhere to do

spy
a secret agent who gathers information

superhuman
stronger or faster than an ordinary human

telepathic
talking to someone using your mind instead of your mouth

villain
a bad person who causes trouble

Index

Africa 20

Ant-Man 16-17

Asgard 14

Ashen Combine 26

Atlantis 24

Banner, Bruce 18

Barnes, Bucky 32

Barton, Clint 28

Belova, Yelena 34

Black Panther 6, 20-21, 26

Black Widow 28, 34-35

Captain America 6, 8-9, 10-11, 26

Captain Marvel 7, 12-13

Danvers, Carol 12

Doctor Doom 24, 36, 42-43

Earth 6, 14, 20, 28

Eternal Titan 40

Fantastic Four 36-37

Hawkeye 28

Hulk 7, 18-19

Human Torch 36-37

Impossible City 26

Invisible Woman 36-37

Iron Man 29, 45

Lang, Scott 16

Loki 14, 38-39

Mister Fantastic 36-37

Mjolnir 14

Namor 24-25

North Atlantic Ocean 24

Pym, Hank 16

Redwing 10

Rogers, Steve 6, 8-9, 32

Romanoff, Natasha 28, 34-35

Shang-Chi 6, 22-23

Stark, Tony 29

T'Challa 20

Thanos 24, 40-41

Thing 36-37

Thor 6, 14-15, 38

Thunderbolts, the 30-31, 32, 34

Wakanda 20

Wilson, Sam 7, 9, 10-11

Winter Soldier 31, 32-33

White Widow 31, 34

 Quiz

Are you an Avengers expert? Try the quiz to find out!

1. What is Carol Danvers's Super Hero name?

2. Which Avenger can fly with the help of his hammer?

3. Who does Sam Wilson have a special connection to?

4. What team does the White Widow join?

5. Which villain wears a mask to hide his face?

1. Captain Marvel 2. Thor 3. Redwing 4. The Thunderbolts
5. Doctor Doom